Creative Drama
and Musical Activities
for Children

Also by Robina Beckles Willson

For Younger Readers

THE SHELL ON YOUR BACK

WHAT A NOISE!

For Older Readers

THE VOICE OF MUSIC

ROBINA BECKLES WILLSON

Creative Drama and Musical Activities for Children

Improvised movement, games,
action songs, rhymes, and playlets

Illustrated by
GUNVOR EDWARDS

790.192

Publishers   PLAYS, INC.   Boston

[C 1977]

Text Copyright © Robina Beckles Willson 1977

Illustration Copyright © William Heinemann Ltd 1977

First American edition published by
PLAYS, INC. 1979

Library of Congress Cataloging in Publication Data

Willson, Robina Beckles.
Creative drama and musical activities for children.

'Published in Great Britain under the title Musical merry-go-round'

1. Games with music. 1. Singing games. 3. Play-party.
4. Children's plays. I. Edwards, Gunvor. II. Title.

M1993.W73M9   1979   780   78-23275
ISBN 0 8238 0230 2

Printed and bound in Great Britain

To Catherine,
with love

Introduction

The aim of this book is to give to the parent, teacher or playgroup leader material for introducing very young children to music and the enjoyment it can bring. He or she will not need to be a specialist or an instrumentalist, but will be able to adapt the ideas, stories and rhymes set out here to suit the size and ages of the group, his own skills and the equipment and space available.

At a very young age children can begin to enjoy making and observing sounds, stopping and starting sounds, hearing and joining in rhythm and tunes. A musical response is awakened by such awareness, and the elements of music can be woven into their stories, games, rhymes, and topics of everyday interest.

Music can be an all-embracing experience. Children can create music with their own voices: speaking, shouting, whispering, singing, humming, whistling. They can make home-made sound-makers and begin to use traditional instruments. They can provide sound effects for stories and invent tunes for rhymes. And they can move to music, by walking, running, marching, dancing, hopping, galloping, jumping, skipping, swinging, stretching and pretending to ride.

They will come to discover music in the voices of animals and birds and in everyday sounds, and to notice rhythm in working machines. The widest range of music, from ancient to classical, to jazz and pop, can be played to them, from radio and record, to give them a foretaste of the immense variety which is part of their heritage.

At the end of the book you will find a list of useful books and records, and also an index which includes all the contents under various activity headings.

Robina Beckles Willson

A Quartet of Musical Games

It is easier for judging to use a radio or record player to provide the music.

Musical Bumps

While the music is played, the children prance and dance about. As soon as it stops, they must bump down to the ground. The last one down is out. The last remaining child is the winner in this and the other three games.

Musical Chairs

A row or rows of chairs or cushions are put out, one less than the number of children playing the game. When the music begins, the children walk round the chairs. As it stops, each child tries to find a seat. The one left standing is out.

Musical Statues

The children dance about to the music and when it stops each 'freezes' in a pose, like a statue. The first child to move or wobble is out. Then the music starts again.

Musical Mats

The children circle the room, singly or in twos, jumping over a mat on their way, while the music plays. When the music stops the last person to have jumped over the mat is out.

Traditional Skipping Rhymes

One, two, three, four
Jenny at the cottage door.
Five, six, seven, eight
Eating cherries off a plate.
O. U. T. spells out!

When I was in the kitchen,
Doing a bit of stitching,
In came a bogey-man
And I ran out!

Jumping and Clapping Rhymes

Teddy bear, Teddy bear, touch the ground.
Teddy bear, Teddy bear, turn right round.
Teddy bear, Teddy bear, show your shoe,
Teddy bear, Teddy bear, that will do.

The woods are dark;
The grass is green;
Here comes Johnnie
With his tambourine.

Question and Answer in Rhyme and Rhythm

The class or group can be divided into two facing each other, or answer the reader's questions. Answering obliges the children to listen to the questions and come in on time.

Question	*Answer*
One two,	Buckle my shoe.
Three four,	Knock at the door.
Five six,	Pick up sticks.
Seven eight,	Lay them straight.
Nine ten,	We'll start again.
	(Last time: A big fat hen.)

"What's your name?"	"Sarah Jane."
"Where do you live?"	"Down the lane."
"What's your number?"	"Cucumber."
"What's your town?"	"Dressing-gown."

"What's your name?" "Mary Jane."
"Where do you live?" "Down the lane."
"What do you keep?" "A little shop."
"What do you sell?" "Ginger pop."
"How many bottles do you "Twenty-four, now go
sell in a day?" away."

"Rat a tat tat, who is "Only Grandma's pussy-
that?" cat."
"What do you want?" "A pint of milk."
"Where's your money?" "In my pocket."
"Where is your pocket?" "I forgot it."
"O, you silly pussy-cat!"

Riddles, Dipping, Choosing, Counting, Racing

Do you like apples?
Do you like pears?
Do you like tumbling down the stairs?

Do you like white?
Do you like pink?
Do you like falling in the sink?

Ickle ockle blue bockle
Fishes in the sea.
If you want a pretty maid
Just pick me.

Both hands are presented clenched and the child has to guess in which hand is the object. Hide a pebble in your hand and chant the rhyme.

Handy pandy, sugary candy
Which will you have?

or   Handy dandy riddledy ro,
      Which hand will you have, high or low?

Each child presents two clenched fists, which are tapped by the counter. On the word 'more', the tapped fist is withdrawn. The winner has the last fist left.

One potato, two potato, three potato *four*,
Five potato, six potato, seven potato *more*.

For Starting Races All Together
Ready, Steady, Go

One to make ready,
And two to prepare.
Good luck to the rider
And away goes the mare.

Bell horses, bell horses,
What time of day?
One o'clock, two o'clock
Time to go away.

Rhymes for Chanting and Action and Stopping

Children can enjoy the pleasure of moving to the rhythm of these rhymes. Gradually they will learn to control their movements and to stop and start sounds and actions on time.

A Farmer Went Trotting

Actions

For 'Bumpety, bumpety, bump': the children should kneel then sit back and bounce on their feet.

For 'Lumpety, lumpety, lump': the children should clap with cupped hands, which means three big claps, or thuds on the floor.

Or the story could be mimed and shakers used to emphasize the refrain's rhythm.

A farmer went trotting upon his grey mare,
   Bumpety, bumpety bump!
With his daughter behind him so rosy and fair,
   Lumpety, lumpety lump.

A raven cried, "Croak!" and they all tumbled down,
   Bumpety, bumpety bump!
The mare broke her knees and the farmer his crown,
   Lumpety, lumpety lump.

The mischievous raven flew laughing away,
   Bumpety, bumpety bump!
And vowed he would serve them the same the next day,
   Lumpety, lumpety lump.

Hoppity

A. A. MILNE

Encourage the children to join with the reader on the
'hoppities' and count them along their fingers, with the
'hop' reaching the thumb, to get the number right. They
could also tap or shake shakers to the rhythm as different
children take their turn to hop, eg "Jonathan Harper
goes . . ." See if anyone can hop the whole rhyme without
changing feet.

Or the whole group could hop while clapping, or a
'rhythm group' could provide the beat for the rest.

Christopher Robin goes
Hoppity, hoppity,
Hoppity, hoppity, hop.
Whenever I tell him
Politely to stop it, he
Says he can't possibly stop.

If he stopped hopping, he couldn't go anywhere,
Poor little Christopher
Couldn't go anywhere . . .
That's why he *always* goes
Hoppity, hoppity,
Hoppity,
Hoppity,
Hop.

Song on a See-saw

Titty cum tawtay
 The ducks in the water
Titty cum tawtay
 The geese follow after.

Swan swam over the sea
Swim, swan, swim!
Swan swam back again.
 Well swum swan.

Rhyme for Being a Monkey on a Rope, Jumping Along

Addy-addy – on – kon – kay
Addy-addy – on – kon – kay
Addy-addy – on – kon – kay
Tippy over.
(The monkey does a somersault.)

This Old Man

English Folk Song for Counting

The children can tap with hands or clap with clappers to the 'nick-nack'. They might also enjoy rolling over at the end of each verse, then sitting up for the next, finally subsiding on the last refrain, pretending to be worn out or fast asleep.

This old man, he played two,
He played nick-nack on my shoe;
Nick-nack, etc.

This old man, he played three,
He played nick-nack on my tree;
Nick-nack, etc.

This old man, he played four,
He played nick-nack on my door;
Nick-nack, etc.

This old man, he played five,
He played nick-nack on my hive;
　　Nick-nack, etc.

This old man, he played six,
He played nick-nack on my sticks;
　　Nick-nack, etc.

This old man, he played seven,
He played nick-nack down in Devon;
　　Nick-nack, etc.

This old man, he played eight,
He played nick-nack on my gate;
　　Nick-nack, etc.

This old man, he played nine,
He played nick-nack on my line;
　　Nick-nack, etc.

This old man, he played ten,
He played nick-nack on my hen;
　　Nick-nack, etc.

The Three Billy-goats Gruff

The children can join in the story together, all taking the various parts, or four groups could practise each part separately, then put them into the story. When they know the story well, four children could mime the action, and the story could be reduced to the sounds of the goats' hooves and the Troll's three questions. Their answers could then be supplied by the whole group with the reader pointing cues to make the timing work. The skeleton version would help them to stop and start sounds as 'conducted' by agreed signs by the reader.

Sounds

'Trit-trot'	Quiet tapping with the finger nails
'Clip-clop'	Knocking with the knuckles
'Clitter-clatter'	Stamping with feet on the floor

Voices

"Who's that tramping over my bridge?"	The Troll shouting The Troll growling
"It's only me, the smallest Billy-goat Gruff."	High whisper
"It's only me, the second Billy-goat Gruff."	Ordinary voice
"It's only *me*, the biggest Billy-goat Gruff."	Fierce voice

Once upon a time there were three Billy-goats called Gruff. They lived in the country and roamed about, looking for fields where the grass grew green and juicy. Grass was their favourite food, and when they ate a lot of it they grew sleek and fat.

One day they ran down a stony field and saw a river. Across the river was a beautiful field of juicy green grass. And there was a wooden bridge over the river.

"How lovely it would be to cross that bridge and eat and eat that grass," said the smallest Billy-goat Gruff. "I'm hungry."

"The trouble is," said the biggest Billy-goat Gruff, "that a wicked old Troll guards that bridge. He's like an ugly giant. And he catches anybody who tries to cross his bridge and gobbles them up."

"He won't catch me!" said the youngest Billy-goat Gruff.

And before they could stop him, he ran to the wooden bridge and began to trot across.

"Trit-trot. Trit-trot. Trit-trot." (*Sound*)

Before he was half-way across the wooden bridge, the great big Troll came swooshing up out of the water and clambered up on to the bridge, blocking the way across.

"Who's that tramping over my bridge?" he roared. (*Growl*)

"It's only me, the smallest Billy-goat Gruff," he whispered.

"I'm going to catch you," roared the Troll.

"Oh don't catch me. I'm so small and thin, I'm not

worth catching. Wait for a bigger Billy-goat Gruff and see what he's like. Look, over there!"

And the smallest Billy-goat Gruff ducked under the Troll's giant legs before he could bend down and catch him. Then he ran over the bridge straight on to the field of juicy green grass.

"Trit-trot. Trit-trot. Trit-trot." (*Sound*)

Now when the second Billy-goat Gruff saw his little brother enjoying the juicy green grass he said, "If he could get over the bridge, then so could I."

So he went running down to the wooden bridge and began to clip-clop across with his bigger hooves.

"Clip-clop. Clip-clop. Clip-clop." (*Sound*)

Before he was half-way across the wooden bridge the great big Troll came swooshing up out of the water and clambered up on to the bridge, blocking the way across.

"Who's that tramping over my bridge?" he roared. (*Growl*)

"It's only me, the second Billy-goat Gruff," he said.

"I'm going to catch you," roared the Troll.

"Oh don't catch me. I'm so small and thin, I'm not worth catching. Wait for a bigger Billy-goat Gruff, and see what he's like. Look over there!"

And the second Billy-goat Gruff dodged round the Troll's giant legs before he could bend down and catch him. Then he ran over the bridge, straight on to the field of juicy green grass.

"Clip-clop. Clip-clop. Clip-clop." (*Sound*)

Now when the biggest Billy-goat Gruff saw his two younger brothers enjoying the juicy green grass, he said, "If they could get over the bridge, then so could I."

So he went running down to the wooden bridge and began to clitter-clatter across with his big hooves.

"Clitter-clatter. Clitter-clatter. Clitter-clatter." (*Sound*)

Before he was half-way across the wooden bridge, the great big Troll came swooshing up out of the water and clambered up on to the bridge, blocking the way across.

"Who's that tramping over my bridge?" he roared. (*Growl*)

"It is *me*, the biggest Billy-goat Gruff," he shouted.

"I'm going to catch you," roared the Troll.

"No you are *not*," shouted the biggest Billy-goat Gruff. "I am going to catch *you*."

And he waved his big horns in the air. Then the biggest Billy-goat Gruff clitter-clattered straight at the Troll and butted him hard with his horns. He pushed the Troll so hard that he fell off the bridge and into the water with a giant splash. The Troll sploshed into the deep, deep water, and was never seen again.

Then the biggest Billy-goat Gruff ran over the bridge straight on to the field of juicy green grass.

"Clitter-clatter. Clitter-clatter. Clitter-clatter." (*Sound*)

"I have got rid of the wicked old Troll," said the biggest Billy-goat Gruff to his brothers. "Now anyone will be quite safe to cross that bridge, whenever they want to do so."

"All I want to do," said the smallest Billy-goat Gruff, "is to eat and eat this juicy green grass until I am as big and brave as you."

Home-Made Musical Instruments and Sound-Makers

Making instruments will encourage children to observe sounds. There is good scope for their own ideas and improvisations.

Let them collect and hoard containers and any material which may be suitable. Home-made instruments enable each child to have something to play. Many sound-makers can be made with little help, and used immediately by everybody, or in groups.

The following suggestions are arranged in order of what is probably easiest to do: Shaking, Striking, Scraping, Plucking and Blowing.

27

Shaking

Rattle a bunch of keys on one ring.

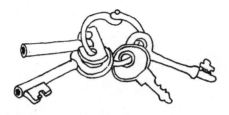

Thread buttons of wood, metal or plastic (not covered) loosely on string, and rattle them. Three or four big ones can be cupped in the hand and shaken. Or play on the buttons with the fingers while the loop of string is wound round the hand.

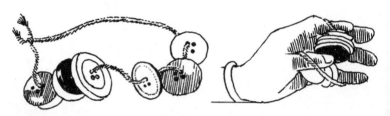

Make a large enough hole in foil milk bottle tops for them to move easily when threaded on string. Then shake about a dozen together.
Put about a dozen foil milk bottle tops in a thin plastic bag with room to rattle about. Fasten the top and shake.

Thread three or four metal curtain rings on string and shake them.

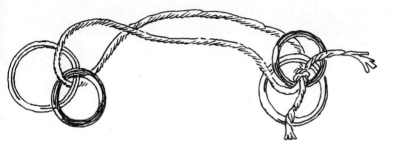

Hold several postcards at one corner and shake them. This gives a good flapping noise.

Hold two wooden or old metal spoons by their handles, one between middle and index finger, the other between the index finger and the thumb. Shake them so that the spoons' bowls clash against each other.

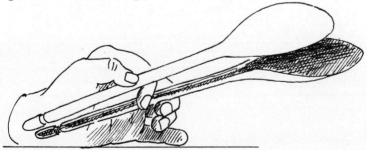

Container Shakers

The principle is to have a firm container and put in various fillings to gain different sounds. Children can bring in containers and experiment.

Some Containers: Plastic or metal boxes and tins with lids that can be sealed with sticky tape if necessary. Plastic bottles. Plastic or metal soap-savers. Roughly matching limpet shells which can be taped together.

Some Fillings: Rice, dried peas, big seeds, small nails, metal paper clips, beads, pebbles.

Striking

Beaters
The simplest beaters are wooden, metal or plastic spoons, but a ball of papier mâché built up on a wooden rod or a wire whisk from the kitchen can be tried out. For a softer beater try a piece of polystyrene or a cork fixed on a rod of thin dowel, or a kitchen bottle brush.

Chiming
Let children find out by experimenting that things struck must be free to vibrate, and that touching them with the hand will mute the sound. The wall bracket or saucepan lid demonstrate this well.

Nails make good chimes and sound different notes. Tie a loop of string or wool round six-inch (15-cm) 'wires' or four-inch (10-cm) 'cuts' (the names of useful nails for this purpose). Then hold them up and tap them with a spoon or another nail. Or tap a suspended fork. A nail collection can be set in a frame or a box.

A metal coat hanger will chime if it is hung by a piece of string and tapped with a metal beater.

Strike a large metal wall bracket, about eight or ten inches (20–25 cm) size, hung on a string with metal, and it will make a resounding chime.

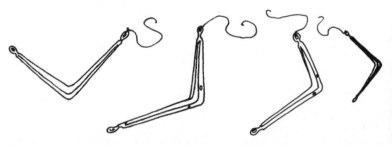

Hold a frying pan by its handle and strike the edge with the side of a wooden spoon to make it chime. A big pan will make a low gong. A flattish saucepan lid will also chime well if held by the knob.

Tap foil or enamel plates and tin trays with various beaters.

Thread metal curtain rings and string them out, then tap them with a metal tea spoon for a delicate chime.

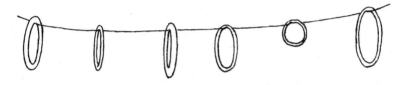

Clonking
Ask a butcher to cut out some short rib bones of beef. Scrub and wash them well, then dry them if possible in the sun for the marrow to dry out and the bones to become hollow. Round off the ends with sand paper.

Hold one bone in one hand and tap it across the top with another bone. If the hand is big enough, the pair of rib bones can be held between the fingers and clonked against each other. (If there is one finger between the bones, they will sound a higher tone than if there are three.)

Or two pieces of one inch dowel, ten or twelve inches (25–30 cm) long and rounded off with sand paper will make good rhythm sticks.

33

Blocks of wood can be clapped together, or date box lids, which are thin wood and easy to hold.

Coconut shells clonk well, and so do plastic cream or yoghurt pots, or plastic lids from bottles. Walnut shells make a crisp sound too.

Drumming
First of all children can try simply thumping with flat hands or clenched fists and stamping with their feet to music, or chanting or singing.

They can also experiment with empty tins, tapping them with fingers or beaters. Cylinders often sound best on their sides.

A large coffee or cocoa tin with a plastic lid is a versatile drum, because the child can bang the metal end or thrum on the plastic. Wearing a metal thimble on one finger gives variety of tone.

More Fragile Instruments
If conditions are suitable, it is possible to get good chiming from tapping suspended clay flower pots (with thick string knotted at the holes), mugs or cups, with wooden spoons. Experiment with water and bottles and glasses. (See p. 67)

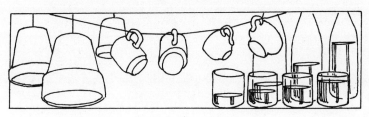

Scraping

Scrape plastic or foil ridged containers with finger nails or a thimbled finger.

Draw a finger nail or a spoon across corrugated cardboard.

Rub against each other sticks or blocks on which coarse sand-paper has been glued or pinned.

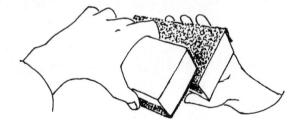

Draw a metal nail firmly over the turns of a long metal screw, which makes a satisfying rasp.

Push a metal thimble up and down on a metal grater. The sound is harsh, but may be enjoyed.

Plucking

Fix rubber bands round an open box. Stop them slipping by cutting little grooves. Try out different sizes of box and thicknesses of rubber band. Pluck with fingers or a match stick.

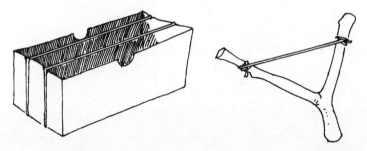

Dry out a chicken or turkey wishbone, then loop a thin rubber band across the opening, and tighten by winding it over. Then pluck it. Other versions of this strummer can be made with Y-shaped sturdy twigs.

Blowing

Fold a piece of greaseproof or waxed paper over the teeth of a comb. Then hum through the paper, moving it slightly from side to side and not getting it wet. Bigger teeth will vibrate more easily than small.

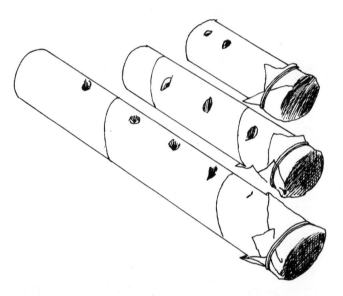

Humming, singing, whistling and saying noises like 'too – too' reverberate well through cardboard tubes, which have been stiffeners. Make a hole or holes near the blowing end of the tube, and try covering and uncovering them with the fingers. Try someone holding a piece of greaseproof paper up against the end of the tube as it is blown, and it will make a sound more like a humming kazoo.

Then fasten a piece of greasproof paper tautly over the non-blowing open end, and secure it with a rubber band. Long tubes produce effective noises, almost like Wagnerian tubas.

Staple a semi-circle of thin cardboard into a cone-shaped trumpet into which a child can hum or make sounds whose quality is changed.

Cut drinking straws (preferably of paper, not plastic) at each side into a wedge shape. Blow through the wedge gently. Shorten the straw to change the note.

A Noise Box

Try and build up an ever changing collection of these materials for children to play with from a Noise Box. They will take enormous pleasure in sounds they have discovered for themselves and in naming instruments they reckon they have invented.

Using the Instruments

The first skill is to make the instrument sound. The next is to be able to make it sound to order, to time, and to stop sounding. Give each child a striker of some kind and let him practise. Then, to get everyone playing together, say the words:

Bom tiddly batch cake, brown bread,

and each child tries to play the two notes on 'brown bread,' in rhythm and at no other time. It is quite hard to do this with a large group. Try conducting the two notes, and get the players to watch you. Turn your back and make them do it by ear only, following your words.

Vary this with:

I tiddly I tie, pom pom.

Try it loudly and softly, while still keeping in time.

The two notes are crotchets, and you can, if these are already being introduced, point them out as 'walk-walk' notes, then change to 'run-run', 'walk', quaver-quaver crotchet, by playing 'currant bread'.

Bom tiddly batch cake, currant bread.

(For striking in time and counting, practise the clock striking. See p 89.)

Use skipping chants and other rhymes which have a good beat to clap or beat in time. (For example See p. 10)

Let children make long sounds and short sounds,stopping the vibration with the hand (see p 31). And, similarly, let them listen to and identify long and short, loud and soft sounds, then make those with their strikers.

Percussion sounds are satisfyingly easy to produce. Children can also say quickly what *kind* of a sound they are playing.

Also let them learn silence (rests), holding their instruments quiet for say two beats, *then* playing again.

The Animals Went in Two by Two

Traditional Song for Counting and Acting

The an-i-mals went in two by two, Hurrah!___ Hurr-ah!___ The an-i-mals went in two by two, Hurr-ah!___ Hurr – ah!___ The an – i-mals went in two by two, The el – e-phant and the Kan-ga-roo, And they all went in-to the ark, For to get out of the rain. __

The animals went in two by two, Hurrah!
                                                                Hurrah!
The animals went in two by two, Hurrah!
                                                                Hurrah!
The animals went in two by two,
The elephant and the kangaroo,
And they all went into the ark,
For to get out of the rain.

The animals went in three by three . . .
The wasp, the ant and the bumble bee . . .

The animals went in four by four . . .
The great hippopotamus stuck in the door . . .

The animals went in five by five . . .
By eating each other they kept alive . . .

The animals went in six by six . . .
They turned out the monkey because of his tricks . . .

The animals went in seven by seven . . .
The little pig thought he was going to heaven . . .

Animal Noises: a Game and a Song

Grunt, Piggy, Grunt

One child is blindfolded. All the others sit down in a circle. The blindfolded child moves towards another child and sits by him, or on his knee, saying: "Grunt, piggy, grunt." Then he has to guess from the grunts who the 'piggy' is. If he guesses right, that child is blindfolded next, and everyone moves place in the circle.

Variations can be invented, like "Poor Pussy, Miaow".

Old MacDonald Had a Farm

For other verses: ducks, quack-quack; turkeys, gobble-gobble; lambs, baa-baa; dogs, woof-woof; cats, miaow-miaow; pigs, hoink-hoink.

From **Teapots and Quails**

EDWARD LEAR

This can be said at a learner's pace for children learning to hop. Those who can manage that can try changing legs and hopping backwards, all in time to the rhyme.

> Tadpoles and Tops
> Teacups and Mops
> Set him a hopping
> and see how he hops!

> Saucers and Tops
> Lobsters and Mops
> Set it a hopping
> and see how he hops!

Charley

This can be mimed by two children, or acted out in pairs. The clout could be worked out harmlessly, or converted to a smacking sound.

> Charley, Charley,
> Stole the barley
> Out of the baker's shop.
> The baker came out
> And gave him a clout
> Which made poor Charley hop.

The Noble Duke of York

This can be chanted for plain marching in time using any drums or clappers available. A hill can be chalked or marked out on the floor.

Oh the noble Duke of York
He had ten thousand men.
He marched them up to the top of the hill
And he marched them down again.
And when they were up, they were up,
And when they were down, they were down
And when they were only half-way up,
They were neither up nor down.

A Traditional Animal Song
for Chanting

I had a cat and the cat pleased me,
I fed my cat by yonder tree;
    Cat goes fiddle-i-fee.

I had a hen and the hen pleased me,
I fed my hen by yonder tree;
    Hen goes chimmy-chuck, chimmy-chuck,
    Cat goes fiddle-i-fee.

I had a duck and the duck pleased me,
I fed my duck by yonder tree;
    Duck goes quack, quack,
    Hen goes chimmy-chuck, chimmy-chuck,
    Cat goes fiddle-i-fee.

I had a goose and the goose pleased me,
I fed my goose by yonder tree;
    Goose goes swishy, swashy,
    Duck goes quack, quack,
    Hen goes chimmy-chuck, chimmy-chuck,
    Cat goes fiddle-i-fee.

I had a sheep and the sheep pleased me,
I fed my sheep by yonder tree;
    Sheep goes baa, baa,
    Goose goes swishy, swashy,
    Duck goes quack, quack,
    Hen goes chimmy-chuck, chimmy-chuck,
    Cat goes fiddle-i-fee.

I had a pig and the pig pleased me,
I fed my pig by yonder tree;
    Pig goes griffy, gruffy,
    Sheep goes baa, baa,
    Goose goes swishy, swashy,
    Duck goes quack, quack,
    Hen goes chimmy-chuck, chimmy-chuck,
    Cat goes fiddle-i-fee.

I had a cow and the cow pleased me,
I fed my cow by yonder tree;
    Cow goes moo, moo,
    Pig goes griffy, gruffy,
    Sheep goes baa, baa,
    Goose goes swishy, swashy,
    Duck goes quack, quack,
    Hen goes chimmy-chuck, chimmy-chuck,
    Cat goes fiddle-i-fee.

I had a horse and the horse pleased me,
I fed my horse by yonder tree;
    Horse goes neigh, neigh,
    Cow goes moo, moo,
    Pig goes griffy, gruffy,
    Sheep goes baa, baa,
    Goose goes swishy, swashy,
    Duck goes quack, quack,
    Hen goes chimmy-chuck, chimmy-chuck,
    Cat goes fiddle-i-fee.

I had a dog and the dog pleased me,
I fed my dog by yonder tree;
    Dog goes bow-wow, bow-wow,
    Horse goes neigh, neigh,
    Cow goes moo, moo,
    Pig goes griffy, gruffy,
    Sheep goes baa, baa,
    Goose goes swishy, swashy,
    Duck goes quack, quack,
    Hen goes chimmy-chuck, chimmy-chuck,
    Cat goes fiddle-i-fee.

Maresydoats

A Squashed-up Rhyme

Maresydoats
And Doesydoats
And Littlelambsytivy.
A Kiddlytivytoo,
Wouldn't you?

This comes from:

Mares eat oats,
And does eat oats,
And little lambs eat ivy.
A kid'll eat ivy too,
Wouldn't you?

A Home-Made Band

The following home-made instruments are used, or others can be substituted:

Chime with wooden spoon and saucepan lid
Clappers with two flat pieces of wood
Gong with spoon and round tin tray
Scraper rasp with ridged foil vegetable box or similar
    packing
Bongo with coffee tin with plastic lid
Comb and greaseproof or tissue paper
Clapper with two yoghurt or similar plastic pots
Rattle with mustard tin with dried peas inside and lid
    taped on

Then to the music of 'She'll Be Coming Round the Mountain', a traditional American song, each instrument is introduced:

I'll be clapping on my clappers . . .

I'll be gonging on my go-ong . . .

I'll be scraping on my scraper . . .

I'll be bonging on my bongo . . .

I'll be blowing comb and paper . . .

I'll be clonking on my clonker . . .

I'll be rattling on my rattle . . .

Finally, when the band is complete:

We'll be called the Home-Made Band
                        when we come . . .

If I Were Not at School Today

This is a song which can be a game with the children making their own variations. Depending on their skill and invention, the teacher can give them ideas, or draw them from the children. One child can mime what he wants to be, and the rest can guess what it is or copy the action. While the 'solo' is sung, the others could hum.

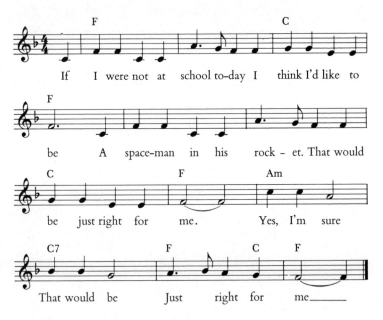

Variations A lady in the sweet shop. A gardener in the garden. A cook making cakes. A boxer in the ring. A footballer on the field. A milkman in his float. A pop singer with his guitar. A window cleaner up his ladder. A driver driving a train. A policeman on his motor bike. A mummy or a daddy with a baby. A postman with his letter-bag.

Hopscotch

This is a traditional counting and jumping game. The children, watching and waiting impatiently for their turns, count and clap.

Chalk out this pattern of numbers. A child throws a stone to land in square one, hops up the numbers, jumping with two feet on two and three, five and six, eight and nine, and turns round, hopping on ten. The child must not hop in the square where the stone has landed, but must stoop and pick up the stone on the return journey down the numbers.

Now the child throws the stone into the second square. The next child has a go when the first falls, or makes a mistake, or the stone does not land in the appropriate square. The first child to have worked his way up and down wins.

Skip to my Lou or Shoo-li-loo

AMERICAN FOLK SONG ADAPTED AND ARRANGED BY
JOHN A. AND A. LOMAX

This song can be turned into a variety of games. One
child can skip in the centre of a circle while the others sing
and clap to the verse. During the chorus, he chooses a
partner to skip with him. At the end of the chorus he
rejoins the circle and his partner skips round inside.

Children can skip in a circle in pairs.

2. I'll get another one, prettier'n you,

3. Going to market two by two,

4. Can't get a red bird, a blue bird'll do,

5. Fly in the sugar bowl, shoo, fly, shoo,

6. Skip a little faster, that won't do,

Traditional Skipping and Counting Rhymes

Children can make up their own tunes to these rhymes.
(See also p 40.)

Inter, mintery, cutery, corn,
Apple seed and briar thorn;
Wire, briar, limber lock,
Five geese in a flock,
Sit and sing by a spring
O-U-T and in again.

Inter, mitzy, titzy tool,
Ira dira, dominu,
Oker, poker, dominoker,
Out goes you.

In pin,
Safety pin,
In pin OUT!

Twist about, turn about,
Jump Jim Crow;
Every time I wheel about
I do just so.

Chanting for Taking Turns and Finishing First

First the worst,
Second the best.
Third the one with the hairy chest.
Fourth the one with the angels' wings.
Fifth the one that sings and sings.

Another Skipping Rhyme

This can be used for skipping with a rope, or with a long loop of elastic round two chairs or the ankles of two children (elastic or French skipping). Or two children could face each other and clap out the rhythm on their hands.

> The Johnsons had a baby
> They named him Tiny Tim
> They put him in the bath tub
> To see if he could swim.
>
> He drank up all the water
> He ate up all the soap!
> He tried to eat the bath tub
> But it wouldn't go down his throat.

"Momma, Dadda, I feel ill.
Call the doctor round the hill."

In came the doctor.
In came the nurse.
In came the lady with the alligator purse.

"Doctor, doctor, will I die?"
"Yes my son, but do not cry.
Shut your eyes and count to ten."
(*Shut eyes*)

One, two, three, four, five, six, seven,
eight, nine, ten.

Out went the doctor.
Out went the nurse.
Out went the lady with the alligator purse.

The Boy and the Wizard

This story is based on Goethe's ballad, 'The Pupil in Magic' and Dukas' Scherzo, 'The Sorcerer's Apprentice'.

Joining in the Story
Children can make up their own magic words and spells, once the story is familiar. Water sounds can be provided (see p 67).

The Wizard's spell: Aygo paygo tarragarra
                      Tarragarra tarragoo
The Boy's spell: Iffay, offay, pinkety thumb
                      The broom shall make the water
                      come
The Boy's wail: Stop, broom, stop, broom, stop,
                      broom, stop.

The Broom's work: Run tip splosh. Run tip splosh.
Run tip splosh.
The story can be mimed to Dukas' music, with three main parts or groups, the Boy, the Wizard and the Broom.

Once upon a time a Boy was living with a Wizard, helping with all the work in his palace. The Boy did not like work much, but he did like watching magic spells.

The Wizard was a marvellous magician. He made it all look so easy. And each day, when the jobs were done, the Wizard taught the Boy some magic, easy little tricks to begin with, like making flowers open and shut to magic orders.

But the Boy wanted to do magic tricks that would save him doing any hard work in the palace. He really was rather a lazy boy.

So he decided to learn the magic words the Wizard said, which was not very easy, as sometimes he whispered:

"Aygo paygo tarragarra
Tarragarra tarragoo."

Sometimes he shouted:

"Aygo paygo tarragarra
Tarragarra tarragoo."

Sometimes he said the magic words very slowly, over and over again.

"Aygo . . . paygo . . . tarragarra . . .
Tarragarra . . . tarragoo . . . Aygo paygo . . ."

Sometimes he said them very fast indeed:

"Aygopaygotarragarratarragarratarragoo."

And the Wizard never got the words in a muddle, as the Boy did, when he practised the spell or had to say it very slowly:

"Aygo . . . paygo . . . tarragarra . . .
Tarragarra . . . tarragoo."

He tried the spell very fast:

"Aygopaygotarragarratarragarratarragoo."

Nothing happened.

"I must watch and listen again," thought the boy. "If I keep trying, I'm sure I'll be able to do big tricks like him."

So one day, when the Wizard had left him in charge of the palace, the Boy decided to try out some real magic on his own.

The Wizard had told the Boy to fetch water from the well. Usually the Boy had to carry heavy buckets from the well to fill up a water tub in the palace.

"Today," said the Boy to himself, "someone else is going to do the work. By my magic. Stand up, broom. Grow a head and legs and arms and hands. You do my water carrying for me."

The boy said the magic words he had heard the Wizard say for this job:

"Iffay, offay, pinkety thumb
The broom shall make the water come."

When he had said this the broom jumped up and grew a head and legs and arms and hands. It ran to the well, picked up two buckets, filled them and ran back to the palace. Then it tipped the water, splosh, into the tub.

The Boy was delighted. "Look at my magic. I needn't do anything," he said.

The broom went on working: *Run, tip, splosh. Run, tip, splosh. Run, tip, splosh.*

Soon the tub was full.

"You can stop now," said the Boy. "Stop, broom, stop, broom, stop, broom, stop."

But the broom did not stop. It went on working. *Run, tip, splosh. Run, tip, splosh. Run, tip, splosh.*

The water began to drip over the edge of the tub, then to trickle over the floor. The broom went on working: *Run, tip, splosh. Run, tip, splosh. Run, tip, splosh.*

The water was getting deeper. It was up to the Boy's ankles. He could not remember the magic words to stop the broom fetching water: *Run, tip, splosh. Run, tip, splosh. Run, tip, splosh.*

"I'll stop you somehow," shouted the Boy. He ran and

got an axe and chopped the wooden broom in two.

But then the *two* parts of the broom both went on working with *their* arms and legs: *Run, tip, splosh. Run, tip, splosh. Run, tip, splosh.* So now twice as much water was being poured into the palace from four buckets, faster and faster.

The boy shouted again, "Stop, broom, stop, broom, stop, broom, stop!"

But the brooms went on working: *Run, tip, splosh. Run, tip, splosh. Run, tip, splosh.*

The water was creeping up the stairs.

Suddenly there was a loud voice shouting; louder than the Boy's wailing, louder than the brooms' running or the water's sploshing.

The Boy's master, the Wizard, was back.

The Boy was so worried that he did not notice that the Wizard had said the spell backwards. But the brooms noticed. They dropped the buckets, and joined together to make one broom again. And the water noticed, and started rolling down the stairs, then ran bubbling all the way back to the well.

"Those who do magic," said the Wizard, "must be able to un-do magic. If you start magic, you must be able to stop it too."

"I think," said the Boy, "that I'll start work instead. I've had enough magic for one day. I'll learn my spells the slow way after all."

Water Music

Watery sounds are easy to reproduce. Take small glass bottles of the tonic water or Coca-Cola size, jam jars and drinking glasses. Fill the bottles to where they begin to taper and half fill the other containers.

Children can tap the outside of the glasses with wooden pencils, noting the different notes which chime if the amount of water is varied. Or, using plastic straws, they can blow bubbles into a bottle, a glass and a jam jar, noting the different sounds.

Rilloby-Rill

HENRY NEWBOLT

The rhythm of this poem can be enjoyed by clapping or
tapping or beating, and joining in the repeated refrains.
Four children can mime the grasshoppers fiddling in time
to the rhythm, and others can be sulky fairies.

Grasshoppers four a-fiddling went,
    Heigh-ho! never be still!
They earned but little towards their rent
But all day long with their elbows bent
    They fiddled a tune called Rilloby-rilloby,
    Fiddled a tune called Rilloby-rill.

Grasshoppers soon on Fairies came,
    Heigh-ho! never be still!
Fairies asked with a manner of blame,
  "Where do you come from, what is your name
    What do you want with your Rilloby-rilloby,
    What do you want with your Rilloby-rill?"

"Madam, you see before you stand,
    Heigh-ho! never be still!
The Old Original Favourite Grand
Grasshoppers' Green Herbarian Band,
    And the tune we play is Rilloby-rilloby,
    Madam, the tune is Rilloby-rill."

Fairies hadn't a word to say,
    Heigh-ho! never be still!
Fairies seldom are sweet by day,
But the Grasshoppers merrily fiddled away,
    Oh, but they played with a willoby-rilloby,
    Oh, but they played with a willoby-will!

Fairies slumber and sulk at noon,
    Heigh-ho! never be still!
But at last the kind old motherly moon
Brought them dew in a silver spoon,
    And they turned to ask for Rilloby-rilloby,
    One more round of Rilloby-rill.

Ah, but nobody now replied,
    Heigh-ho! never be still!
When day went down the music died,
Grasshoppers four lay side by side.
    And there was an end of their Rilloby-rilloby,
    There was an end of their Rilloby-rill.

From **Teapots and Quails**

EDWARD LEAR

If each verse is said twice, the child can suit the action to
the words.

Ribands and Pigs
Helmets and Figs,
Set him a jigging,
and see how he jigs!

Sofas and Bees
Camels and Keys
Set him a sneezing
and see how he'll sneeze!

Wafers and Bears,
Ladders and Squares
Set him a staring
and see how he stares!

Hurdles and Mumps
Poodles and Pumps
Set it a jumping
and see how he jumps!

A Tongue Twister

Moses supposes his toeses are roses
But Moses supposes erroneously;
For nobody's toeses are posies of roses
As Moses supposes his toeses to be.

Rhyme

Eenie, meanie miney mo,
Catch a chicken by his toe,
If he squeals, let him go.
Eenie, meanie, miney mo.

Song

As I was going along, long, long,
A-singing a comical song, song, song,
The lane that I went was so
                  long, long, long,
And the song that I sung was as
                  long, long, long,
And so I went singing along.

Hiccup

I beg your pardon, Mrs. Arden,
There's a kitten in your garden,
Eating of a 'mutting' bone,
    It's nutting
    If you don't say mutting.

Nonsense Songs

This song is probably over a hundred years old, and other versions are known. Children can invent their own tunes to these rhymes, or chant in unison.

> Coymee nayro
> Kil too kayro
> Coymee nayro coymee
> Pim strim
> Strumadiddle
> Lara bone a ring ting
> A ring num
> Bulledim a coymee.

This was sung to a child in Jamaica, a long time ago.

> I went down town, down Central Street,
> Sing-song kitchi kitchi kymeeo
> There's where the people grow big feet,
> Sing song kitchi kitchi kymeeo.
> Keemo kymo dahro wah,
> M'hi m'ho m'rumpsi pummydiddle
> Soup cat nib cat
> Sing song kitchi kitchi kymeeo.

The second half of this song should be chanted faster and faster, but without tripping over the words.

Weather Chants

Rain, rain, go away,
Come again another day.

Rain, rain, go away,
Come again on Saturday.

Rain, rain, go away,
Don't come back till Christmas Day
Little Arthur wants to play.

Rain, rain, go to Spain,
Never show your face again.

Rain on the green grass and rain on the tree
And rain on the housetops but not on me.

Rain, rain, pour down,
But not a drop on our town.

It's raining, it's pouring;
The old man's snoring;
He got into bed
And bumped his head,
And couldn't get up in the morning.

Snow, snow, faster,
Alley, alley, baster.

Alley, alley, baster,
Come down faster.

Experiment to make rain sounds with light-weight rattles, or drop grains of rice on to foil. Try half the children whispering the words 'pitter-patter' and the other half 'patter-pitter'.

The North Wind Doth Blow

For the wind, children can either use home-made sound effects (see p. 38), or combine in groups, making such noises as 'ooh, eeh', blowing and trying to whistle before each verse.

They can also mime: the robin hiding his head, the swallow flying away, the dormouse rolled in a ball, and the children jumping about, changing at the wind sound. Or they can be in five groups: wind, robin, swallow, dormouse and children.

> (*Wind sound*)
> The north wind doth blow,
> And we shall have snow,
> And what will the robin do then, poor thing?
> Oh, he'll go to the barn
> And to keep himself warm
> He'll hide his head under his wing, poor thing.

> (*Wind sound*)
> The north wind doth blow,
> And we shall have snow,
> And what will the swallow do then, poor thing?
> O, do you not know
> He's gone long ago
> To a country much warmer than ours, poor thing?

> (*Wind sound*)
> The north wind doth blow
> And we shall have snow,
> And what will the dormouse do then, poor thing?

Rolled up in a ball,
In his nest snug and small,
He'll sleep till the winter is past, poor thing.

(*Wind sound*)
The north wind doth blow,
And we shall have snow,
And what will the children do then, poor things?
O, when lessons are done,
They'll jump, skip and run,
And play till they make themselves warm, poor things.
(*Wind sound, dying away.*)

Windy Nights

ROBERT LOUIS STEVENSON

The galloping rhythm of this poem can be accentuated
with coconut shells, walnut shells, yoghurt pots or plastic
bottle caps. Or the tongue can be clicked on the roof of
the mouth. The children can practise making the galloping
sound come and go. For wind noises they can say 'sssh',
then whistle into a toilet roll tube; (however breathy, it's
quite a good sound).

Whenever the moon and stars are set,
    Whenever the wind is high,
All night long in the dark and wet,
    A man goes riding by.
Late in the night when the fires are out,
Why does he gallop and gallop about?

Whenever the trees are crying aloud,
    And ships are tossed at sea,
By, on the highway, low and loud,
    By at the gallop goes he.
By at the gallop he goes, and then
By he comes back at the gallop again.

The Emperor and the Nightingale

ADAPTED FROM HANS ANDERSEN

Joining in the Story

The bells	Jingle bells or small chimes
The nightingale's song	Chooc chooc, pioo pioooo (A crescendo can also be tried on this song.)
Clock chiming seven	Chimes
Clapping with hands	
Key winding	Say 'weech', or use rasp to give turning sound
The clockwork nightingale's song	Tweet tweet, tweet tweet, said very strictly in time without expression

80

Long long ago the Emperor of China lived in a beautiful palace. All round the palace was a beautiful garden full of flowers and blossoming trees. And the garden did not only look beautiful: it sounded beautiful too. The Emperor's gardeners had tied little bells to the flowers and trees so that in the gentlest breeze bell sounds echoed through the grass and the flowers and the trees (*bell sounds*).

But the most beautiful sound of all was the song of the nightingale. This little brown bird hopped among the bushes dipping his reddish tail. With a flit and a flutter he began to sing:

"Chooc chooc, pioo pioooo."

His song became famous and people came from all over the world to hear him sing.

"Chooc chooc, pioo pioooo."

One day the Emperor was giving a party in his palace and he decided that the nightingale should sing to his guests.

"Go and tell the nightingale to come and sing here

tonight at seven o'clock," he told his minister.

So the minister hurried through the garden to find the nightingale. He did not notice the pretty flowers or the tinkling bells (*bell sounds*). He was too busy looking for the little reddish brown bird, who was shy and hard to find.

At last he came to the tree where the nightingale best liked to sing, hidden among the leaves.

"Your Emperor commands that you come to his palace to sing for his guests, tonight at seven o'clock," said the minister.

"If that is what the Emperor wishes, I shall come," said the nightingale. "But in the day or the night I do sing best in the garden."

That night at seven o'clock, all the guests had arrived for the Emperor's party. As the clock struck seven (*chimes*), the nightingale flew in from the garden and perched on the window-sill.

With a flit and a flutter he began to sing:

"Chooc chooc, pioo pioooo."

All the guests were delighted and clapped (*clapping*), for

the nightingale did sing such a beautiful song: he sang so many notes and made an astonishing noise for such a little bird. The guests kept asking for more. And again with a flit and a flutter he began to sing:

"Chooc chooc, pioo pioooo."

They clapped again (*clapping*), and he sang until he was tired.

The Emperor said, "I shall keep this wonderful nightingale in a cage here in my palace. And then he can sing for me any time I wish."

"I do like best your garden and your trees," said the tired nightingale. "But if my Emperor wishes it, then I shall stay here."

So the nightingale was put into a golden bird cage, and fell asleep straightaway, while the Emperor's guests danced and ate all through the night.

For many days the nightingale lived in the cage by the window, sadly looking out over the palace gardens. But each time he was asked, with a flit and a flutter he sang for the Emperor.

"Chooc chooc, pioo pioooo."

Then one day the Emperor received a present from the Emperor of Japan. It was another bird in a gold cage decorated with sparkling diamonds, rubies and other jewels. And this bird was covered with jewels too and made of gold. For he was not a real nightingale, but a clockwork bird.

When he was wound up with a golden key (*weech*), there was a little click. Then up and down went his stiff metal wings, and he sang, "Tweet tweet tweet – " and went hop hop hop.

His song was not half as beautiful as the real nightingale's, but the minister said:

"Now we have this bird he can sing at any time we wind him up. He'll never get tired like the little brown nightingale does. We don't need him any more."

So they opened the cage, and let the real nightingale fly out of the window, away back to the garden and the trees. He knew that his song was much better than the clockwork song, but he did not mind. He was so pleased to be free. He flew amongst the green leaves. He felt the fresh breeze on his feathers, and heard the little bells ringing on the flowers (*bell sounds*). Then with a flit and a flutter he began to sing, louder and louder with delight.

"Chooc chooc, pioo pioooooo." (*crescendo*)

Many years passed and the Emperor was an old man and became ill. Lying in bed, he remembered the song of the nightingale and asked to hear it.

"Certainly," said the minister, and wound up the clock-work bird with the golden key (*weech*). But the clockwork bird was old too, and it gave a little click and slowly lifted its metal wings just once up . . . and . . . down. Then it sang just once, "Tweet," and stopped.

"It has broken. I am afraid it cannot sing any more," said the minister.

The Emperor lay sadly in bed. The garden bells were too far away for him to hear. All he wanted to hear was the song of the nightingale.

Suddenly there was a flit and a flutter on the window sill. The real nightingale perched there and began to sing:

"Chooc chooc, pioo pioooo."

As he sang, the song was so beautiful the Emperor began to feel better. As the nightingale went on singing, the Emperor sat up in bed for the first time for many days.

"I feel better every minute that I hear that song," said the Emperor. And the bird even saw tears in his eyes. "How

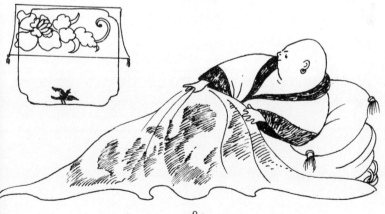

can I repay you for making me well again? Choose any treasure you wish for."

"All the reward I want is to see my Emperor well again," said the nightingale.

"Stay with me for ever, so that I may hear your song," said the Emperor. "I will have the most beautiful cage in the world made for you to live in."

"I beg that you will never shut me in a cage again," the nightingale replied, "but let me live free in the gardens of your palace. If I am free I promise I will come and sing for you every evening of my life."

And so he did. Every evening, while the clockwork bird stood stiffly and silently in his golden cage, the real nightingale came from the garden to the palace. With a flit and a flutter he began to sing:

"Chooc chooc, pioo pioooo."

And the nightingale and the Emperor lived for many happy years, one in the palace and the other in the garden.

Listen to bird sound records.

Robins and Wrens

The children can try whistling and miming the movements
of the robin and the wrens at the appropriate times.

> Little Robin Redbreast
> Came to visit me.
> This is what he whistled
> Thank you for my tea.

> Little Robin Redbreast
> Sat upon a rail;
> Niddle noddle went his head,
> Wiggle waggle went his tail.

> As little Jenny Wren
>   Was sitting by the shed,
> She waggled with her tail
>   She nodded with her head;
> She waggled with her tail,
>   She nodded with her head,
> As little Jenny Wren
>   Was sitting by the shed.

> There were two wrens upon a tree,
> Whistle and I'll come to thee;
> Another came, and there were three,
> Whistle and I'll come to thee;
> Another came and there were four,
> You needn't whistle any more,
> For being frightened, off they flew,
> And there are none to show to you.

Planting Rice

FOLK SONG FROM THE PHILIPPINES ARRANGED BY
JOHN M. KELLY JR.

In Asia rice is often planted in groups or families. The planters work in long rows, stooping to push the seedlings into the mud, first to one side, then to the other. Rice is a grass and the seedlings are transplanted to swampy fields when they are about six inches high.

Children can act out this work song as they sing.

Plant-ing rice is ne-ver fun, Work from morn till set of sun, Can-not sit and can-not stand, Plant the seed-lings all by hand. Plant-ing rice is no fun, Work from morn till set of sun, Can-not sit, Can-not stand, Plant the seed-lings all by hand...

Clocks and Chimes

Clocks

Ask the children to listen to all the clocks and watches there
are to hand, so that they become aware of the different
paces of ticking. It is also useful to have children practise
some ticking sounds.

The children can swing themselves slowly from side to
side from the waist upwards for a big pendulum:
Ticker-tocker, ticker-tocker . . .

For an ordinary clock, they can nod their heads fairly
quickly in time to the sound: ticky-tock, ticky-tock, ticky-
tock . . .

For a watch, fast little movements can be made, with
four fingers of one hand bunched and tapping on the
thumb of the other hand: tick-tack, tick-tack . . .

Chimes

These may be made by striking any or all of the following: suspended earthenware flower pots, angle brackets, tubular metal, enamel plates, metal forks, xylophones, chime bars (see p 31).

It is worth using chiming the hours when learning to tell the time. It is good practice for the reader to show how many hours to chime by holding up the appropriate number of fingers to each chimer, or to all the children. Or one child can be a cuckoo and hide, until summoned to pop out through a door or opening to say, "Cuckoo," for each hour.

> What's the time?
> Half past nine.
> Hang your breeches on the line.
> What's the time?
> Half past ten.
> Time to put them on again.

Listen to the second movement of Haydn's 'Clock Symphony'.

Birthday Chimes

Children's birthdays can be celebrated by chiming the number of years.

> Happy birthday to you.
> Happy birthday to you.
> Happy birthday, dear Rachel,
> Happy birthday to you!   (*Chimes*)

Or the birthday boy or girl can sound out the number of years on a drum or piano, or whatever he or she chooses, while the others count aloud.

Pick a Bale of Cotton

AMERICAN FOLK SONG ADAPTED AND ARRANGED BY
JOHN A. AND ALAN LOMAX

This is an old work song from the days of slavery. In fact, a bale of cotton weighs five hundred pounds, and no one has ever really picked that much in a day. The cotton flower is followed by a pod or boll, which, when ripe, bursts open and shows down, which is 'snatched' by the picker. He bends over the cotton plants; the bolls are thorny; he is dragging a sack behind him. This song is to keep him going, cheer him up.

The children can imitate this work.

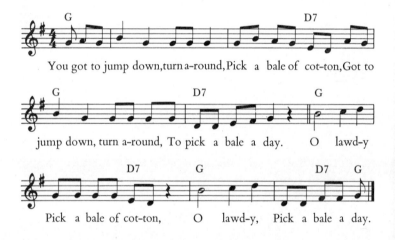

You got to jump down, turn a-round, Pick a bale of cot-ton, Got to jump down, turn a-round, To pick a bale a day. O lawd-y Pick a bale of cot-ton, O lawd-y, Pick a bale a day.

2. (In pairs) Me an' my pardner can
Pick a bale of cotton,
Me an' my pardner
Can pick a bale a day.
Chorus.

92

3. (In pairs) Me an' my wife can
    Pick a bale of cotton
    Me an' my wife
    Can pick a bale a day.
    Chorus.

Dustbin Song

TRADITIONAL

As this song has a strong beat, it is good for beating triple time (three beats in a bar), with any clanging beater.

Don't put your muck in   my dust-bin, my dust-bin my dust-bin.

Don't put your muck in   my dust-bin, My dust-bin's full.___

Goodbye to a Greedy Dragon

ROBINA BECKLES WILLSON

Joining in the Story

The following sounds can be said, or supplemented by real hammers, pans and drums, signalled by the reader, and cued by the text.

The carpenter	Hammer-bang
The cook	Clisher-clash
The soldiers	Stamper-stomp
The drummers	Booma-boym
The children	"Dragon, dragon, go away."

The single listener will have to try making enough din for several people!

Once upon a time there was a dragon, who left his own land of the dragons because he was too lazy to work. He went and stayed just outside a village, and shouted every morning:

"I am hungry. Where's my food?"

The people in the village were a bit frightened of him

94

because he was so big and green, with enormous wings and a long, long tail!

The wise woman of the village told them, "This dragon is not really fierce, you know. He's just greedy and lazy."

"All the same, we'd better feed him," said the people. "If we don't, he might come and grab our food, and trample all over our houses and gardens with his great big feet."

So every time the dragon shouted, "I am hungry, where's my food?" the villagers carried along dozens of loaves of bread, baskets of apples, potatoes and carrots, big hunks of meat and long strings of sausages.

The dragon ate them all up very fast. He did not get hiccups, but he did breathe out some fire and smoke before he rolled over and went straight off to sleep.

Each day the dragon shouted, "I am hungry, where's my food?"

He was eating so much that the villagers did not have enough food for themselves.

"What can we do?" they asked the wise woman. "The dragon is getting fatter and fatter, but we are getting thinner and thinner."

"He must be sent away," said the wise woman. "He must go back to his own land of the dragons. You must frighten him away."

"What us? He's ten times bigger than our biggest man," said the villagers. "He could blow us over with his hot breath."

"Try and wake him up with noise," said the wise woman. "Dragons don't like loud noises, and this dragon, remember, likes to sleep all day."

"We could try some noise," said the villagers.

So the next morning, the village carpenter went and watched the dragon eat ten loaves of bread, one basket of

potatoes, and twelve eggs, in their shells. Then the dragon was so full of food that he blew out some fire and smoke, rolled over and went straight off to sleep.

Then the carpenter crept out as near to the dragon as he dared, and began to hammer nails into a big piece of wood. *Hammer-bang, hammer-bang* he went, as hard as he could.

Hammer-bang. Hammer-bang. Hammer-bang. Hammer-bang. At last the dragon opened one eye.

"Did I hear a tapping?" he murmured, then rolled over and went straight back to sleep.

The carpenter went back to the wise woman.

"I wasn't loud enough," he said. "The dragon only woke up for a minute, then just went back to sleep."

"You must get some help," said the wise woman.

So the carpenter asked a cook to come and help him by banging with his pots and pans. When they got as near to the dragon as they dared, the carpenter went *hammer-bang*, while at the same time the cook went *clisher-clash* with the saucepan lids.

Hammer-bang. Hammer-bang.
Hammer-bang. Hammer-bang.
Clisher-clash. Clisher-clash.
Clisher-clash. Clisher-clash.

At last the dragon opened one eye.

"Did I hear a tapping?" he murmured, then rolled over and went straight back to sleep.

"We still weren't loud enough. He only woke up for a minute," said the carpenter and the cook, and went to get some more help.

This time, they asked some soldiers to march right by the dragon. They marched as near to the dragon as they dared, and stamped on the ground. *Stamper-stomp. Stamper-stomp.*

At the same time the carpenter went *hammer-bang*, and the cook went *clisher-clash*; all together.

> *Hammer-bang. Hammer-bang.*
> *Hammer-bang. Hammer-bang.*
> *Clisher-clash. Clisher-clash.*
> *Clisher-clash. Clisher-clash.*
> *Stamper-stomp. Stamper-stomp.*
> *Stamper-stomp. Stamper-stomp.*

At last the dragon opened *two* eyes.

"Did I hear some tapping?" he murmured. But he rolled over *again* and went straight back to sleep.

"We *still* weren't loud enough. He only woke up for a minute," said the carpenter and the cook and the soldiers, and they went to get some more help.

This time they asked the soldiers' drummer, and he came marching as near as he dared to the dragon, going *booma-boym* on his drum.

At the same time the carpenter went *hammer-bang*, the cook went *clisher-clash* and the soldiers went *stamper-stomp*, all together.

Hammer-bang. Hammer-bang.
Hammer-bang. Hammer-bang.
Clisher-clash. Clisher-clash.
Clisher-clash. Clisher-clash.
Stamper-stomp. Stamper-stomp.
Stamper-stomp. Stamper-stomp.
Booma-boym. Booma-boym.
Booma-boym. Booma-boym.

At last the dragon opened two eyes and got up on his front paws.

"Did I hear some tapping?" he murmured. "I hope it's not going to get noisy round here." But he rolled over *again*, and went straight back to sleep.

"We were nearly loud enough," they said. "We just need to waken him up a bit more. Who would have the loudest voices to *shout* at the dragon?"

"I know," said the carpenter. "We'll ask the children. They are tired of the greedy dragon taking all their food."

So the children from the village came as near as they dared to the dragon, and shouted, "Dragon, dragon, go away."

At the same time the carpenter went *hammer-bang*, the cook went *clisher-clash*, the soldiers went *stamper-stomp* and the drummer went *booma-boym*; all together.

Hammer-bang. Hammer-bang.
Hammer-bang. Hammer-bang.
Clisher-clash. Clisher-clash.
Clisher-clash. Clisher-clash.
Stamper-stomp. Stamper-stomp.
Stamper-stomp. Stamper-stomp.
Booma-boym. Booma-boym.
Booma-boym. Booma-boym.
Dragon. Dragon. Go a-way.

And *this* time the dragon opened both his eyes, got up

on his front paws, then his back paws.

"What is this horrible noise?" he bellowed. "Can't a dragon have a bit of rest?"

Nobody answered him. They could hardly hear him. They were making so much noise, all together.

Hammer-bang. Hammer-bang.
Hammer-bang. Hammer-bang.
Clisher-clash. Clisher-clash.
Clisher-clash. Clisher-clash.
Stamper-stomp. Stamper-stomp.
Stamper-stomp. Stamper-stomp.
Booma-boym. Booma-boym.
Booma-boym. Booma-boym.
Dragon. Dragon. Go a-way.

The dragon was too fat to fly, too fat to run either, but he did start waddling away, with his long green tail between his legs.

"I'm going back to my old job in dragon land," he said. "There's far too much noise around here for me."

When he had gone away, the villagers went home in procession for a big tea, with the wise woman leading, waving her hands in time. Behind her the carpenter was going *hammer-bang*, the cook going *clisher-clash*, the soldiers going *stamper-stomp*, the drummer going *booma-boym*. (*Reader point to each to give noise.*)

And at the end of the long line the children were saying:

"Dragon, dragon, go away!
Don't come back another day!"

And he never did.

Calico Pie

EDWARD LEAR

Recite this and the children can join in the chorus as they pick it up. Try whispering the last chorus almost as an echo.

Calico Pie,
The little Birds fly
Down to the calico tree,
Their wings were blue
And they sang 'Tilly-loo'—
Till away they all flew,
And they never came back to me!
They never came back!
They never came back!
They never came back to me!

Calico Jam,
The little Fish swam
Over the syllabub sea,
He took off his hat
To the Sole and the Sprat,
And the Willeby-wat,—
But he never came back to me!
He never came back!
He never came back!
He never came back to me!

Calico Ban
The little Mice ran,
To be ready in time for tea,
Flippity Flup
They drank it all up,
And danced in the cup,—
But they never came back to me!
They never came back!
They never came back!
They never came back to me!

Calico Drum,
The Grasshoppers come,
The Butterfly, Beetle and Bee,
Over the ground,
Around and around,
With a hop and a bound,
But they never came back!
They never came back!
They never came back!
They never came back to me!

Circle Song

From Melodies: Extract III

LEWIS CARROLL

The children can make two circles, and in one pace to the rhyme, growing shorter and shorter, while in the other they grow taller and taller.

> There was once a young man of Oporta
> Who daily got shorter and shorter,
>   The reason he said
>   Was the hod on his head,
> Which was filled with the *heaviest* mortar.

> His sister, named Lucy O'Finner,
> Grew constantly thinner and thinner;
>   The reason was plain,
>   She slept out in the rain,
> And was never allowed any dinner.

Ring Song and Game

The children sit in a circle and hold a long string threaded through a ring, then knotted. One child stands in the middle and watches the other children's hands on the string as they secretly pass the ring along. When the song stops, the child has to guess which hand is holding the ring. If he is right, the holder takes his place in the centre.

Who'll come in to my lit - tle ring To make it a lit - tle big - ger? My lit - tle ring, My lit - tle ring, Who is ___ hold-ing my lit - tle ring?

The Bee who Seemed Furious and Angry

ROBINA BECKLES WILLSON

The children can make buzzing and humming noises, starting and stopping to order. They can get louder and softer to order, as the bee comes and goes. It might also be useful to observe and mention the sounds of flies', daddy-long-legs', and moths' flapping wings, and possibly the whining noise of mosquitoes.

"Someone," said the Bee,
"Has taken my honey.
And is having it now for his tea.
It makes me feel angry,
Furious and angry,"
Rumbled and bumbled the Bee.

So do not be curious
When a Bee appears furious,
But leave him alone without fuss.
For the next thing he does,
When he's had a long buzz,
Is to make some more honey for us.

A Weather Rhyme

If bees stay at home,
Rain will soon come;
If they fly away,
Fine will be the day.

Listen to the 'Flight of the Bumble Bee', by Rimsky-Korsakov.

I Sent a Letter to my Love

A Singing Game

The children sit in a circle. One is chosen to run outside the ring carrying a handkerchief which he drops at the end of the song. The child who finds the handkerchief behind him picks it up and runs round the ring in the opposite direction. The child first back at the space takes it, and the other one runs round outside as the game is repeated.

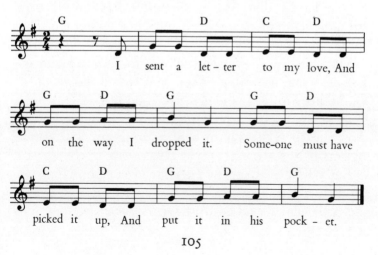

Good Morning and Good Night

ROBINA BECKLES WILLSON

Joining in the Story

Footsteps	Wooden blocks, clonked together
Knocking	
Thud	Something heavy dropped on the floor
Miaows	
Birdsong	Whistling, or say words such as 'cherp, cheep, chissick chissick'.
Telephone ringing	Say 'ring-ring', or imitate with a chime
Fly zooming	Zzzz, zzzz

It would also be enjoyable for Jim's actions to be mimed by a child.

Once upon a time a man came home from work. And he began to make his breakfast. Not his tea, because he had been working all night. He had been driving a train from Scotland to London. And by the time he had walked home from the station it was seven o'clock in the morning, time for his breakfast.

The train driver, whose name was Jim, cooked his breakfast, ate it and washed up. Then he stretched and yawned.

"I think I'm ready for my bed," said Jim.

So he got ready for bed just as you do at the end of the day, and soon he was in bed, wearing red and purple pyjamas.

But as soon as he shut his eyes there were footsteps down his garden path (*blocks*). There was a rat-a-tat on the door (*knocking*) and a thud on the floor (*thudding noise*).

"Only the postman," said Jim and turned over and tried to go to sleep.

But as soon as he shut his eyes there were more footsteps down his garden path (*blocks*), and whistling then another thud on the floor (*thudding noise*).

"Only the paper boy," said Jim, and turned over and tried to go to sleep.

But as soon as he shut his eyes there were lots of footsteps on the pavement outside his house (*blocks*).

"Only the children going to the bus stop to go to school," said Jim, and turned over and tried to go to sleep.

But as soon as he shut his eyes there were more footsteps on his garden path (*blocks*), and a clanking noise of bottles.

"Only the milkman," said Jim, and turned over and tried to go to sleep.

But as soon as he shut his eyes there was another sound:

"Miaow. Miaow. Miaow."

"Oh dear," said Jim. "I forgot to feed the cat. And she's been out all night as well as me. I'll get no peace until I do." (*more miaows*)

So he got up and opened the back door, to let the cat in. As he did so, some sparrows perched on his roof began a loud song:

"Cherp cheep, chissick chissick."

"Could you please sing a bit softer? I'm going to bed," said Jim.

He gave the cat her breakfast and went back to bed.

The cat finished her breakfast and cleaned her face with her paws, then curled herself up comfortably and went straight off to sleep.

But as soon as Jim got back into bed again and shut his eyes, the phone rang:

Ring-ring. Ring-ring. Ring-ring.

He got out of bed again to answer the phone.

"Good morning, Jim. It's the drivers' manager here," said the voice. "Sorry to disturb you, when I expect you're just off to bed, and I should be saying good night!"

"It's all right," said Jim. "I've been to bed twice, but I keep on being woken up, by other people going to their day's work!"

"Then I've good news for you, Jim. I've rung to ask you to work in the days next week, not the nights. Would you like that?"

"I think I would," said Jim. "Then I'd be going to work in the morning with everyone else."

So he went back to bed. But as soon as he shut his eyes there was another sound. *Zzzz, zzzz, zzzz.* Jim opened his eyes. It was a big fly, zooming round the room. Jim watched him crossly. "Noisy little thing," said Jim. Then luckily the fly flew out through the window, and Jim turned over and tried to go to sleep.

And *this* time when he shut his eyes he began to feel sleepy. And he didn't hear the traffic going up and down the road all day. It seemed to fade away. He didn't hear the children running back from school at dinner time (*quick blocks*).

He didn't hear any more noises to keep him awake. Because, just like his cat, Jim was fast asleep.

Joke Lullaby

TRADITIONAL

Good night, sweet repose.
A bunch of fleas around your nose.
Good night, good night.
Mind the fleas don't bite.
If they bite,
Squeeze them tight,
And they won't come back another night.

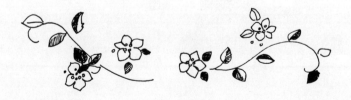

The Cowboy's Dream

AMERICAN FOLK SONG ADAPTED AND ARRANGED BY
JOHN A. AND ALAN LOMAX

The 'dogies' in the chorus are motherless calves, who, eating grass before being old enough to digest it, develop big stomachs. The nickname 'doughnuts' became 'doughies' or 'dogies'.

Children can swing to the rhythm as if riding over the prairie.

Last night as I lay on the prai-rie ⸺ And looked at the stars in the sky ⸺ I won-dered if e - ver a cow-boy ⸺ Would drift to that sweet by and by ⸺ *Roll on, roll on, Roll on lit tle do gies, roll on, roll on. Roll on, roll on, roll on lit tle do gies, roll on.* ⸺

I know there's many a stray cowboy
Who'll be lost at the great final sale,
When he might have gone in green pastures
Had he known of the dim narrow trail.

They tell of another big owner
Who's ne'er overstocked, so they say,
But who always makes room for the sinner
Who drifts from the straight narrow way.

III

"Lazy Mary, Will You Get Up?"

A Singing Game

Lazy Mary (or other name) and her mother are in the
centre of a circle of children. Mary pretends to be asleep
as the children hold hands and walk round her in time to
the song, all singing:—

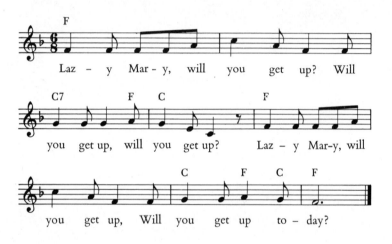

Mary: "What will you give me for my breakfast
                              (or dinner)
         For my breakfast, for my breakfast?
         What will you give me for my breakfast
         If I get up today?"

(One of the children suggests a breakfast.)

Mary: "No mother, I won't get up,
I won't get up, I won't get up.
No mother, I won't get up,
I won't get up today."

Then another suggestion of food can be made, eg Fish
and chips and pink ice-cream, which Mary accepts:

"Yes, mother, I will get up,
I will get up, I will get up.
Yes, mother, I will get up,
I will get up today."

The child whose suggestion Mary accepts takes her
place.

All the Pretty Little Horses

AMERICAN FOLK SONG ADAPTED AND ARRANGED BY
JOHN A. AND ALAN LOMAX

Hush-you-bye, Don't you cry, Go to sleep-y, lit-tle ba - by. When you wake, You shall have All the pret-ty lit-tle hor - ses Blacks and bays, Dap-ples and grays, Coach and six-a lit-tle hor-ses. Hush-you-bye, Don't you cry, Go to sleep-y, lit-tle ba – by, ba – by.

After the words have been sung, the tune of this lullaby can be hummed, and imaginary babies rocked off to sleep.

Rhymes for Night Time and Rest

Go to bed first,
A golden purse;
Go to bed second
A golden pheasant;
Go to bed third
A golden bird.

Up the wooden hill to Bedfordshire,
Down Sheet Lane to Blanket Fair.

God bless this house from thatch to floor,
The twelve apostles guard the door.
Four angels round my bed;
Gabriel stands at the head,
John and Peter at my feet,
All to watch me while I sleep.

How Do You Lie When You Go to Sleep?

ROBINA BECKLES WILLSON

How do you lie when you go to sleep? Go to sleep
Go to sleep. How do you lie when you go to sleep?
go to sleep at bed-time? I lie like_ this when I...

This song would give children the opportunity to show
different ways of settling to sleep. They can be in beds,
bunks or sleeping bags, under traditional bedclothes or con-
tinental quilts, to demonstrate their favourite positions.
Babies are wrapped up in shawls.

Animals' and birds' sleeping habits can also be imitated.
Birds sleep in nests, or tuck their heads under their wings
on a perch. Giraffes sleep standing up, sometimes resting
their necks in the forked branch of a tree. Horses and cows
lie down and roll over. Dogs and cats curl up. In fact, any
pets' sleeping habits can be mimed.

Lullaby

Hush, little baby, don't say a word,
Papa's going to buy you a mocking bird.
If the mocking bird won't sing,
Papa's going to buy you a diamond ring.

If the diamond ring turns to brass,
Papa's going to buy you a looking-glass.

If the looking-glass gets broke,
Papa's going to buy you a billy-goat.

If that billy-goat runs away
Papa's going to buy you another today.

Good Night

Good night
Sleep tight
Wake up bright
In the morning light,
Do do what's right
With all your might.

A Lullaby for the Baby Jesus

'ROCKING', A CZECH CAROL ARRANGED BY MARTIN SHAW

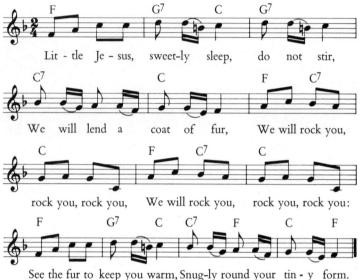

Lit - tle Je - sus, sweet-ly sleep, do not stir,
We will lend a coat of fur, We will rock you,
rock you, rock you, We will rock you, rock you, rock you:
See the fur to keep you warm, Snug-ly round your tin - y form.

Mary's little baby, sleep, sweetly sleep,
Sleep in comfort, slumber deep;
We will rock you, rock you, rock you,
We will rock you, rock you, rock you:
We will serve you all we can,
Darling, darling little man.

Small Sounds Try humming 'Rocking' as well as singing
the words. Ask the children to think about small sounds
which make them sleepy, and contrast them with loud
bangs and thumps which make them wake up and jump,
or move in time. Or encourage the children to notice the
gentle rhythms of lullabies and sway in time.

JUST

ROBINA BECKLES WILLSON

One more rhyme before the musical merry-go-round
stops.

Just one more cake as I finish my tea.
Just one more story to be read to me.

As that was *just* a little bit short,
Would you please read another? I think you ought.

Just a little programme on TV,
I'm sure it's *just* the one for me.

Right round the bath *just* one more swim,
And a hug with the towel as I sit on the rim.

Just one more shadow game on the wall.
Look! Your shadow's terribly tall.

Just a drink of water, a hankie too.
I'm sorry to be such a bother to you.

Just the curtains drawn, and Teddy in bed,
And the covers pulled *just* as far as my head. .

At the stars through the curtains *just* one last peep.
And then I promise
I'll go
Straight
Off
To
Sleep.

A Short List of Useful Books

Buck, Percy, *The Oxford Nursery Book* (Oxford University Press, 1933)

Hunter, Ilene and Judson, Marilyn, *Simple Folk Instruments to Make and Play* (Simon & Schuster, 1977)

Lomax, Alan, *Folk Songs of North America* (Doubleday & Co., Inc., 1960)

Mandell, Muriel and Wood, Robert E., *Make Your Own Musical Instruments* (Sterling Publications Co. Inc., 1957)

Opie, Iona and Peter, *The Oxford Nursery Rhyme Book* (Oxford University Press, 1955)

Seeger, Ruth Crawford, *American Folk Songs for Children* (Doubleday & Co., Inc., 1948)

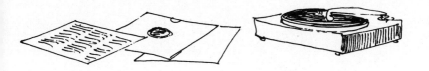

A Short List of Music for Movement

If you have a tape recorder, it is worth taping extracts of music that suggest improvised movement.

Debussy, *The Gollywog's Cakewalk.* From the "Children's Corner Suite." (Children like the syncopated rhythm of this piano piece.)

Delius, *On Hearing the First Cuckoo in Spring.* (This is a quiet piece, to enjoy when resting.)

Dukas, *The Sorcerer's Apprentice.*

Haydn, Symphony No. 101 in D (Clock).

Joplin, Scott, Piano Rags. Joshua Rifkin. (For steady beat.)

Offenbach, *Orpheus in the Underworld.*

Prokofiev, *Peter and the Wolf.* (A story with music.)

Rimsky-Korsakov, *Flight of the Bumble Bee.*

Schumann, Album of Children's Pieces for the Piano. (Several of these are pleasant to dance to, as *The Merry Peasant* and *The Soldiers' March*.)

Tchaikovsky, *The Nutcracker Suite.* (Good for dancing.)

Consult catalogues for recordings of sound effects such as bird and animal noises, bells, clocks, boat whistles, traffic sounds, airplanes, trains, trucks, thunder, common household sounds, etc.

Vivaldi, *The Four Seasons*. Henryk Szeryng, ECO, 6580 002. (The 'Spring' band is good for hopping.)

Collections
Bird Sounds in Close-up, GGL 0483.
Music of the Crusades, Early Music Consort of London, David Munrow, ZRG 673. (The dances have strong rhythms, and the old instruments a fresh sound.)
Songs for Children, arr. Anne Mendoza and Joan Rimmer, ZDA 32. (A good anthology, with percussion and other instruments, of play songs, singing games, folk songs and lullabies.)

Sound Effects
BBC Sound Archives, Davis (Ed.)

No. 1   Weather, Seaside, Bells, Clocks, Babies, Transport   Red. 47M

No. 2   Summer Backgrounds, Horses and Hunting, Children, Crowds, Boats   Red. 76M

No. 4   Domestic Sounds, Doorbells, Clocks, Pets, Traffic, Toys   Red. 104M

No. 5   Transport, Cars, Lorries, Cycles, Cranes, Transport Café   Red. 105M

No. 7   Aircraft, Weather, Crowds, Water, Trains   Red. 113S

As catalogues change so swiftly, it is worth checking with a record and cassette library or dealer when looking for recordings.

Author's Note

Many people have helped me in the preparation of this book, but in particular I should like to thank: Gill Austin of Ronald Ross School, Roehampton; Wendy Bird, Warden of the ILEA Teachers' Centre for Music; Rosemary Davies, Heinemann Young Books; Gunvor Edwards; J. M. Farhall and Mary Willans of Archdeacon Cambridge School, Twickenham Green; J. Hugill, Music Adviser, Richmond-upon-Thames; Jenyth Worsley of the BBC; my daughter Rachel, and her friends.

R. B. W.

Acknowledgements

The author and publishers would like to thank the following for their kind permission to reproduce copyright materials: Methuen Children's Books for 'Hoppity' (p 18) from *When We Were Very Young* by A. A. Milne, illustrated by Ernest H. Shepard, for Canada: Copyright 1924, by E. P. Dutton; renewal, 1952 by A. A. Milne. Reprinted by permission of the publishers, E. P. Dutton; Peter Newbolt for 'Rilloby-Rill' (p 68) from *Poems: New and Old* by Sir Henry Newbolt; Oxford University Press for 'Rocking' (p 118) from *The Oxford Book of Carols*; The Richmond Organization/Essex Music Ltd., London, for 'All the Pretty Little Horses' (p 114), collected, adapted and arranged by John A. Lomax and Alan Lomax TRO – © copyright 1934, 'The Cowboy's Dream' (p 111) collected, adapted and arranged by John A. Lomax and Alan Lomax TRO – © copyright 1938, 'Pick a Bale o'Cotton' (p 92) collected, adapted and arranged by John A. Lomax and Alan Lomax TRO – © copyright 1934, 'Skip to My Lou' (p 56) collected and adapted by John A. Lomax and Alan Lomax TRO – © copyright 1934; Charles E. Tuttle Co., Inc. (Japan) for 'Planting Rice' (p 88) from *Hawaii Sings* by John M. Kelly.

Index

Entries with an asterisk have sound effects suggested.